The Singularity

The Inevitable Intersection of Man and Machine

Table of Contents

Chapter 1. Introduction

In this exciting special report titled "The Singularity: The Inevitable Intersection of Man and Machine", we unravel the elaborate tapestry that threads together technological advancement and human evolution. Although the topic ventures into the intricate realm of science and technology, our narrative remains refreshing and accessible. We delve deep, yet ensure to illuminate the path so the uninitiated don't lose their way. Drawing upon expert opinions, scientific forecasts, and philosophical discourse, we aim to present an intriguing exploration of this inevitable singularity. Be prepared to nurture your curiosity and expand your understanding of the awe-inspiring world that awaits us. Our report works to demystify the confluence of the human intellect and artificial intelligence - a fascinating intersection that might just redefine our notions of existence and reality. Be it out of intrigue, a desire for knowledge or a passion for future-gazing, this special report is an essential addition to your intellectual toolkit.

Chapter 2. A Historical Overview: From Industrial Revolution to AI

In the early 18th century, as steam engines began replacing manual labor, history bore witness to the advent of its first significant technological leap—the Industrial Revolution. The evolution of technology, however, didn't stop there. Herein, we journey through the significant milestones, exploring mankind's ceaseless endeavors to amplify his capabilities using machines.

2.1. The Dawn of Mechanization

The Industrial Revolution, kicking off in Britain around 1760, marked a shift from hand production methods to machines. New chemical and iron production processes emerged, enhancing the rate of manufacturing and enabling large-scale production. The invention of the steam engine by James Watt in 1775 proved instrumental in powering these industrial machines, placing steam power at the center of this transformative era. The advent of mechanization played a pivotal role in shaping economic and societal structures. For the first time, goods production transcended the stringent boundaries of human labor and animal power, paving the way for mass production and a consumer society.

2.2. The Age of Electricity and Steel

The second Industrial Revolution, or the Technological Revolution, initiated around 1870, was characterized by the broad application of electricity and the mass production of steel. Thomas Edison's irreplaceable contributions brought electric power and lighting to homes and factories, marking a significant increase in industrial productivity. Concurrently, the Bessemer Process enabled the mass production of steel, further enhancing industrial growth and catalyzing rapid urbanization. This era brought new technologies, such as the telegraph and railway systems, which revolutionized communication and transportation, effectively shrinking the world.

2.3. The Epoch of Automation

The dawn of the 20th century introduced the third Industrial Revolution, underpinned by the development of electronics, telecommunications, and computers. Henry Ford's assembly line, a paragon of efficiency introduced in 1913, led to the mass production of the automobile and marked the onset of automation. Toward the mid-century, computers began influencing different spheres of human life. The invention of the transistor in 1947 and the integrated circuit in 1958 were transformative, engendering the rise of digital electronics. By 1971, Intel introduced the first commercial microprocessor, leading to the proliferation of personal computers in the subsequent decade.

2.4. Information Technology and the Internet

The late 20th century witnessed a quantum leap in technology with the development of the internet. Innovative satellites and fiber-optics facilitated a global network system, which changed the way we communicate, share, and access information. This was the era of the Information Revolution or Digital Revolution. Data, once scarce, turned into an abundant and vital asset. Technology started shaping human behaviors, cultures, even thoughts. The turn of the century saw the rise of giants like Microsoft, Apple, Google, and Facebook, redefining how humans interact with technology.

2.5. The Emergence of AI

As we navigate the 21st century, the fourth Industrial Revolution emerges, characterized by a fusion of physical, digital, and biological worlds. Artificial Intelligence (AI) and machine learning are taking center stage. Algorithms can now self-learn from data patterns, enhancing their performance over time independent of human intervention. AI has started permeating various fields such as medicine, finance, commerce, and transportation, demonstrating its vast potential. It has also raised profound philosophical and ethical questions regarding machine rights, human identity and the very nature of consciousness, setting the stage for humanity's impending singularity with machines.

In essence, the human journey from the Industrial Revolution to AI is a testament to our innate drive to innovate and transcend existing limitations. It encapsulates our persistent endeavor to augment human potential and broaden the horizons of possibility. However, as we inch closer towards the Singularity, it calls for conscientious deliberation on the repercussions of blending humanity with technology. Just as in previous revolutions, the path forward is fraught with complex challenges, but the horizon promises a future brimming with untapped potential.

Chapter 3. Understanding the Concept: The Singularity Defined

The idea of a singularity, when originated from the realms of mathematics and physics, denotes a point where rules as we know them change or cease to exist, where infinity resides. In the realm of technology and artificial intelligence (AI), the singularity is a prediction, a point in our not-so-distant future where artificial intelligences will surpass human beings as the Earth's most intelligent and capable beings.

3.1. Origins and Understanding

The concept of the singularity owes its genesis to various thinkers, but it is often associated with Ray Kurzweil, a noted futurist and inventor. Kurzweil envisions the singularity as a period of immense technological change, essentially so quick and profound it represents a rupture in the fabric of human history.

In his books, such as "The Age of Spiritual Machines" and "The Singularity is Near", Kurzweil posits that the rate of innovation is accelerating and that "within a few decades, machines intelligence will surpass human intelligence, leading to the Singularity — technological change so rapid and profound it represents a rupture in the fabric of human history".

This underpins the core concept of the singularity – the fact that the progress of technology tends to accelerate because each advancement serves as the platform for the next, creating exponential progress.

3.2. The Asserted Acceleration of Progress

Exponential growth is a hard concept for our human minds to grasp. We are accustomed to linear, step-by-step progress, not the doubling effect that characterizes exponential growth. Let's take Moore's law, the observation that the number of transistors on a computer chip will double approximately every two years. Although this trend is already slowing down with the limits of silicon transistors being reached, it exemplifies how technology can accelerate at an exponential pace.

This relentless doubling and redoubling, turning tiny intervals into vast chasms, is what makes the singularity such a difficult concept and yet it is also what makes it so compelling. Machine intelligence continues to improve, having reached and surpassed human parity in numerous individual tasks, from image recognition to complex games.

But how does relentless technological development lead us to a singularity? The simple answer is that these machines, once reaching a level of superhuman intelligence and capability, may also gain the ability to improve upon their designs or develop new technologies independently without human input.

3.3. Tipping Point: Between Man and Machine

When machines start to improve themselves, using their intelligence which might initially only marginally exceed our own, we may encounter a runaway effect — an intelligence explosion where smart machines start to build even smarter machines. The gap between human and machine capability will abruptly widen into a chasm, marking the tipping point often referred to as the Singularity.

The result of this runaway growth could be machines vastly more intelligent than any human. How much more intelligent? Perhaps as much as a human compares to a snail. And once this explosion is triggered, it's likely we will not have the power to stop or control it.

3.4. Speculations on Timeframes

Predictions regarding when this momentous occasion will occur are a point of contention. Some respected scholars and technologists predict it may happen within this century. Kurzweil, for example, has pinpointed 2045 as the year of Singularity, while others suggest a more precautionary estimate of later this century.

Regardless of the stipulated timeframes, the arrival of the singularity presents both profound opportunities and threats. It represents the prospect of solving entrenched problems, from halting climate change to curing disease. However, it also implies potential hazards, including powerful autonomous weapons or economic disruption on an unprecedented scale.

3.5. Possible Outcomes: Utopia or Oblivion?

The advent of the singularity raises fascinating and problematic questions. What happens in a world where machines surpass humans in intelligence? What does that mean for humanity itself?

The answers, predictions, and theories among scholars vary widely. Some predict a utopia, where AI will eliminate scarcity, leaving us to live in a post-scarcity society where we're free to pursue what we wish. In such a world, physical and mental enhancements could improve life beyond our imagining. AIs would solve problems that humans have been unable to crack, and humans could themselves be augmented with AI capabilities.

Alternatively, there are dystopian views, which include the complete obliteration of the human species either through destructive means or by rendering us redundant. The dangers of a super-intelligent AI, aligned with non-human goals, devastating humanity, have been seriously considered by some of the world's foremost thinkers.

In conclusion, the concept of the Singularity – the point in time when machine intelligence surpasses human intelligence and leads to potentially rapid and profound changes in civilization – is a multifaceted and complex subject. It promises unprecedented rewards and perils. It compels us to confront the fascinating, and at the same time demanding, question of our future relationship with machines. As we edge closer to this supposed event horizon, one thing is clear: We stand on the precipice of a future that is impossible to fully grasp with our current level of understanding.

Chapter 4. Expressions of AI: Current Applications and Capabilities

Artificial Intelligence (AI) has experienced exponential growth and development in the past few years, propelling itself from theoretical calculations to practical applications in seemingly every area of our lives. What began as an interesting concept is now an integral part of our socio-economic fabric, reengineering the way we operate and reshaping our perception of the world.

4.1. Emergence of AI – From Narrow to General Intelligence

The journey of artificial intelligence began with narrow AI, intelligent systems designed to perform specific tasks such as spam filtering, voice recognition, or recommendation systems. These are the AI systems that most of us interact with on a day-to-day basis. An underlying feature of these applications is that they are unable to exceed their pre-defined scope of operation and demonstrate intelligence outside of their designated tasks.

However, the undercurrents of AI research are shifting towards artificial general intelligence (AGI), a type of intelligence that could potentially understand, learn, and apply knowledge across a broad spectrum of tasks, much like a human would. While AGI remains a future vision, its theoretical exploration denotes the next sought-after milestone in our voyage towards the AI-human singularity.

4.2. Unmasking AI – The Ubiquity of AI in Modern Life

Despite the ongoing pursuit of AGI, current AI systems have still managed to embed themselves firmly in our daily lives. They power the recommendation algorithms on streaming platforms, spearhead risk analysis in financial institutions, and even assist in weather forecasting.

More complex iterations of AI allow for impressive feats like real-time language translation, enabling seamless communication across linguistic barriers. AI algorithms also drive the operations of autonomous vehicles, leveraging data from a variety of sensors and assimilating this information to maneuver safely in traffic.

In healthcare, AI is becoming overwhelmingly vital - whether it's in streamlining appointments and administrative tasks, or in the diagnosis and treatment of diseases. AI algorithms are enabling early cancer detection by picking up minute patterns in medical images that may evade the human eye.

Chapter 5. E-commerce and Personalization

One of the most well-known uses of AI is in digital commerce. E-commerce giants utilize sophisticated AI algorithms to provide personalized product recommendations, enhance user experience, manage inventory, and predict trends.

But it doesn't stop there. AI is progressively reshaping traditional brick-and-mortar retail, bringing about 'smart stores' fitted with AI-powered computer vision systems that can track customer movement, behavior, and preferences to augment the shopping experience.

5.1. Advancements in Natural Language Processing

AI's prowess extends to language understanding as well. Technologies powered by natural language processing (NLP) give machines the ability to understand, generate, and respond to human language.

These capabilities underpin numerous applications, from voice-controlled assistants like Siri and Alexa to social media monitoring tools that analyze public sentiment. Modern NLP techniques are also heavily applied in advanced search engines, content suggestions, and automated customer support chatbots.

5.2. AI and Big Data – A Match Made in the Cloud

The sheer amount of data that flows through the digital world is impossible to handle by human standards. Here's where AI comes in, sifting through colossal volumes of data and identifying key insights to help businesses make data-driven decisions. This symbiotic relationship between big data and AI has revolutionized sectors such as healthcare, finance, and transportation, creating an environment where informed decisions are made swiftly and efficiently.

5.3. Vision for the Future – Emerging Applications in Environment and AI Ethics

This rapidly evolving technology is not without its implications. As AI develops and weaves deeper into the fabric of society, questions surrounding AI ethics and regulation have begun to emerge. Concurrently, efforts are underway to harness AI to fight global challenges such as climate change, through approaches like predictive environmental models and sustainability-focused applications.

Conclusively, AI is a central character in the narrative of human evolution, and as we stride towards the singularity, we can only expect its role to become more profound and influential. By acknowledging and understanding its current expressions and capabilities, we can better navigate the future landscape, where the line between man and machine could become increasingly blurred.

Chapter 6. The Singularity's Implications: Promises and Pitfalls

The singularity marks a point in future history where technological growth becomes uncontrollable and irreversible, leading to unfathomable changes in human civilization. Eminent computer scientist Dr. Vernor Vinge, who first popularized the term, suggests it would signify an era where entities with greater than human intelligence might trigger runaway technological growth. Let us venture into this riveting concept and its implications, both promising and perilous.

6.1. Superintelligence and its Precursors

Superintelligence represents an intellect that far surpasses the brightest human minds in practically every aspect, including creativity, general wisdom, and problem-solving capabilities. Some see it as a natural mutation, analogous to the jump from monkeys to humans, but on a significantly condensed timescale. However, reaching this state of superintelligence is not instantaneous, and certain precursors show the gradual progression towards this reality.

Technology has already begun displacing traditional ways of doing things. Automation has morphed into fields once considered human dominions like data analysis, language translation, and even artistic creation. Furthermore, advancements in Machine Learning (ML) and Artificial Intelligence (AI) technologies indicate a shift toward autonomous decision-making capabilities.

6.2. The Promise of Superintelligence

Superintelligence, achieved through artificial means, could have numerous potential benefits. It might solve complex problems that are currently beyond human cognitive capabilities. Devising strategies to mitigate climate change, finding a cure for cancer, or even unraveling the secrets of the universe could become achievable.

Imagine machines predicting natural disasters in advance, or designing cities that perfectly balance human needs with ecological sustainability. Better still, conjure up a scenario where machines devise economic policies that ensure universal prosperity. In essence, superintelligence could make reality of seemingly insurmountable tasks.

6.3. The Pitfalls of Superintelligence

While superintelligence offers potential boons, it also brings a myriad of challenges. In the wrong hands, AI could serve malicious purposes - such as weapons of mass destruction, cyber-attacks, and technological totalitarianism. Even if strictly controlled, superintelligent machines might still constitute threats, especially if they surpass human capability to understand or control.

AI alignment continues to be a major challenge. It describes the difficulty of ensuring that superintelligent AI systems carry out tasks that genuinely benefit humanity, as opposed to inadvertently causing harm due to a misunderstanding of complex human values and emotions.

6.4. The Technological Divide

A major societal concern about the Singularity is the potential creation of a technological divide between those with access to such powerful technologies and those without it. A divide already exists with current technologies, yet the significance of this divide would be far graver in the era of superintelligence.

Moreover, job displacement due to automation and AI is already a concern. With the rise of superintelligence, many fear that a majority of jobs, even those requiring higher education or specialized skill sets, could be automated, leading to serious socio-economic implications.

6.5. Ethics and Philosophy

One of the most profound considerations of the Singularity concerns ethics and philosophy. As we edge closer to creating beings potentially more intelligent than us, the questions posed are paralleled in their enormity. Do these entities possess consciousness, emotions or rights? Would it be ethical to switch off a superintelligent being?

6.6. Looking Ahead

Although predictions about the timeline of the Singularity vary, most agree that its implications would be far-reaching and transformative. As we approach this era, our society must find ways to balance the promising prospects with the associated risks.

Education, policy-making, international cooperation, and foresight would be critical in ensuring that the rise of superintelligence catalyzes human growth rather than destruction. Above all, a sense of collective human responsibility is crucial. Remember, the Singularity may be inevitable, but how we navigate it remains in our hands.

Chapter 7. Transhumanism: The Philosophy of Enhanced Humanity

Technological innovation and human evolution have been deeply entwined for millennia, underpinning much of our progress and shaping our public and private spheres. In the context of the Singularity, one philosophy stands out as central — transhumanism. Transhumanism posits that humanity is not static, but rather on a journey of continuous growth propelled by technological advancements that can push our biological limits.

7.1. Embracing Evolving Human Identity

Since our species' inception, human beings have utilized technology to better understand the world and to improve our circumstances within it. From the creation of fire to the advent of the Internet, our journey has always been one where we've sought to augment our natural abilities, improve our survival rates, and enhance the condition of human life.

Fundamentally, transhumanism espouses the idea that humans should and will continue to incorporate these advancements into the body and mind as a means to reach beyond our natural abilities. It is both a reaction to and extension of the human capacity for adaptability and change. Physical augmentation, cognitive enhancement, and radical life extension are just a few avenues in which transhuman thought sees future potential.

7.2. Physical Augmentation: Rethinking the Body's Limitations

Physical augmentation covers a wide array of interventions aimed at upgrading or enhancing our bodies. This concept is not new—consider glasses that improve our ability to see or a prosthetic limb that allows one to regain mobility. However, the development of technologies that can radically alter human capabilities is quickly advancing from mere speculation to tangible reality.

Nanotechnology, for instance, has the potential to lengthen our lives by targeting disease at the cellular level. Neural prosthetics could potentially cure ailments such as paralysis or motor neuron disease, through directly interfacing with the brain to restore bodily control. In essence, transhumanists foresee a future where we can push beyond our biological limits, transcending the constraints evolution has set upon us.

7.3. Cognitive Enhancement: Upgrading the Mind

Just as with the physical, transhumanism also sees incredible potential in augmenting human cognition. This could be achieved through neurotechnology, pharmaceuticals, genetic engineering, or even the integration of artificial intelligence.

One foreseeable advancement is the use of nootropics, substances that can enhance brain function. We already use caffeine and other natural substances to improve concentration, but there is potential for synthetic drugs that could significantly enhance memory, creativity, or various facets of intelligence.

Moreover, with advancements in brain-computer interfaces (BCIs), there are credible speculations that future technologies may facilitate direct interaction between our brains and computational devices, leading to a dramatic leap in our cognitive capacities.

7.4. Radical Life Extension: Conquering Mortality

Perhaps one of the most radical and controversial aspirations of transhumanism is the desire for radical life extension, even immortality. Researchers are already exploring how aging might be slowed down or reversed at the molecular and cellular levels.

Technologies such as gene therapy, regenerative medicine, and nanomedicine could theoretically repair the cumulative damage done to our bodies over time, fundamentally changing our relationship with aging and death. While the ethical implications are profound, such a shift would undoubtedly redefine what it means to be human.

7.5. Ethical and Existential Considerations

Despite its promise, transhumanism isn't without critics. Ethical issues abound, particularly regarding equitable access to technology and the potentiality for a new form of social stratification between the augmented and the non-augmented. There is also the existential fear that augmentation could diminish our humanity, making us more machine than man.

However, as central as these critiques are, they are considered an integral part of the dialogue within transhumanist thought. The philosophy does not dismiss these issues, it instead challenges us to find solutions. After all, this is quintessential to our spirit: facing the unknown, taking risks, and pushing boundaries to achieve progress.

To fully comprehend the essence of transhumanism, we must entertain the possibility that what it means to be human isn't fixed, but rather an evolving concept — one that is ever-changing based on our alignment and interaction with our technologies. After all, our symbiosis with technology is a testament, not a threat, to our collective survival and continued evolution.

Transhumanism, thus, urges us to aspire to more than what nature has allocated us. The philosophy encourages us to imagine far beyond current human limitations, into a realm where we have the technology to become the main drivers of our own evolution. Ultimate human wellbeing, cognitive liberty, and pursuing lives unfettered from biological constraints are its central tenets — guiding us towards a future where the line between human and machine is less clear, but the promise of progress is unequivocal.

Chapter 8. Economic Impact: How The Singularity Influences Industries

The economic repercussions of the Singularity will be vast and largely unpredictable, potentially leading to paradigm shifts in virtually all sectors of the global economy. By augmenting human intelligence with machine learning and artificial intelligence, man and machine confluence is expected to create a significant economic impact.

8.1. An Overarching Economic Revolution

The Singularity proposes an economic revolution that transcends the confines of specific industries. From agriculture to information technology, transportation to healthcare, every sector of the global economy will experience the impact of this paradigm shift.

Not merely a technological phenomenon, the Singularity will leverage digital capabilities for a profound socioeconomic transformation. Its influence will resonate deeply, fostering new mechanisms of production, innovative business models, and the obsolescence of traditional jobs, thereby generating entirely new employment ecosystems.

8.2. Industry Specific Impact

Expanding upon this concept, it's crucial to understand the broad impact on various industry sectors.

Agriculture, the cradle of human civilization, will experience monumental change as the Singularity influences farming methods. AI-driven predictive farming using data analytics will optimize planting and harvesting cycles, thus increasing food production efficiency.

The industrial sector will increasingly see the deployment of smart factories powered by AI algorithms capable of managing complex manufacturing processes autonomously and with a high degree of precision. This transition could potentially spell the end of traditional factory floor jobs, or herald a new era of machine-human collaboration.

Healthcare transcends mere economic concerns by contributing to our overall quality of life. Machine learning algorithms are already capable of performing medical diagnostics with precision comparable to or exceeding human physicians in certain fields. This could revolutionize healthcare, resulting in improved patient outcomes and cost optimization.

Similarly, transportation and logistics could undergo drastic changes. Technologies like autonomous vehicles and AI-directed supply chains would redefine our understanding of these industries.

Information Technology, the progenitor of the Singularity, will also evolve beyond recognition. Silicon Valley, the hub of tech innovation, may become a digital commune, fostering new technological breakthroughs that push us towards the Singularity.

In short, virtually no industry will emerge from this transformation untouched.

8.3. The Impact on Labor Markets

Notably, the economic repercussions of the Singularity cannot be discussed without addressing labor markets. As machines become increasingly capable of performing tasks traditionally accomplished by humans, questions arise about the future of work.

Increased automation may result in fewer job opportunities in sectors that are easy to automate. However, history teaches us that technology has the propensity to create new jobs as it makes older practices redundant. Therefore, we might envisage an economy where humans and machines work in unison, capitalizing on the strengths of each.

8.4. Redefining Economic Policies

Lastly, the Singularity will necessitate policy changes to accommodate this shift. Governments will have to redefine financial and economic policies, anticipating and mitigating the rise in income inequality that might result from massive shifts in the workforce.

On a macroeconomic level, industries may need to recalibrate their monetary policies to accommodate a potentially inflationary surge in productive capacity. Similarly, fiscal policy may require significant rethinking, as traditional tax bases - particularly income and sales taxes - could dwindle if machines become primary producers. Admittedly, this discussion encourages dialogue on the concept of a Universal Basic Income as a potential panacea, although such propositions are deeply contentious and beyond the scope of this section.

8.5. Conclusion: Embracing Unpredictability

The Singularity's impact on the economy cannot be overstated. Predictably, it introduces considerable uncertainty across sectors. However, by harnessing emerging technologies wisely, societies can capitalize on the opportunities while navigating the challenges that arise in our march towards an interconnected human-machine future. We must collectively approach this rapidly evolving economic landscape with a mix of calculated pragmatism and enthusiastic optimism.

As we stand on the precipice of one of humanity's greatest epochs, the Singularity offers immense potential for economic progress and advancement. In our continuous endeavor for growth and improvement, this unique confluence of man and machine might just be key to propelling us into an era of unprecedented prosperity.

Chapter 9. Legal and Ethical Concerns: Navigating the New World

As society forges headlong into the era of artificial intelligence (AI) and machine learning, it is critical to address the legal and ethical challenges that accompany this pioneering journey. Prudent navigation of this new world is essential, given the profound impact of these technologies on every facet of human existence.

9.1. Legal Implications of AI Integration

As AI becomes increasingly sophisticated, the question of legal responsibility and liability are more relevant now than ever. If an AI, purportedly programmed to operate within the bounds of regulations, commits an offense, who is to be held accountable? The robot? Its creator? Or the operator?

The current legal frameworks are woefully under-prepared to handle the advanced level of automation that AI systems possess. Issues like data privacy, intellectual property, and professional liability, amongst others, need considerable reevaluation and revision.

For instance, the General Data Protection Regulation (GDPR) of the European Union (EU) reframes how personal data can be handled by AI systems. It emphasizes the 'right to explanation', which entitles users to know how decisions that affect them are made by an AI system. However, implementing this right is an extraordinarily intricate task given the opaque 'black box' algorithms that form the core of many AI systems.

In the realm of intellectual property, does an AI have the right to file a patent or copyright? Moreover, who owns the output created by the AI? The algorithm, its creator, or the entity that utilizes the AI?

Professional liability finds itself drowned in a sea of complexities too. If an AI system incorrectly diagnoses a medical condition, who bears the responsibility for the error - the doctor, the hospital, or the AI manufacturer?

9.2. Ethical Implications of AI Integration

While law strives to lay the groundwork for regulating conduct, ethics casts its net wider, encompassing the meticulous process of discerning right from wrong in pursuit of 'the good life'. As AI increasingly becomes entwined in human life, we are compelled to scrutinize it through the ethical lens.

One of the primary ethical challenges is to find equilibrium between security and privacy. While AI can help to enhance security measures, it also possesses the very real potential to breach privacy rights, as exemplified by surveillance technologies.

The question of fairness and bias also looms large. AI systems are known to mirror the biases of their human creators which can result in discriminatory practices. It is essential to determine how we can ensure that AI is free of bias and is used for equitable and reasonable purposes.

Perhaps the most profound ethical issue is defining the rules and limits of AI. What tasks are they permitted to perform? Who decides these parameters and on what basis? How do we prevent misuse of AI? And critically, what becomes of jobs and livelihoods in the wake of automation?

9.3. Regulatory Actions and Considerations

In light of the above issues, regulatory bodies worldwide are hustling to devise comprehensive policies that keep pace with the growth of AI. Concurrently, tech companies and research institutions are also working to lay down ethical standards for AI usage. Their collective aim is to draft regulations which balance innovation with safety and ethics.

The European Union, for instance, has taken several steps forward in this matter. The High-Level Expert Group on Artificial Intelligence, established by the EU, issued guidelines on "Trustworthy AI," emphasizing legal compliance, ethical alignment and robustness as foundational requirements for AI systems.

However, while regulators strive to impose oversight on AI developments, there is a very real danger of stifling innovation. Striking the right balance between fostering growth and minimizing risk is a challenging task that requires careful consideration.

9.4. The Role of the Public

While experts and institutions wrestle with these issues, the role of the general public mustn't be undermined. Their informed consent and understanding is vital to the ethical deployment of AI. Public discourse and education about AI's benefits and pitfalls, its abilities and limitations can help shape a future where AI is an integrated, beneficial, and ethically guided component of our lives.

As we sail into the uncharted waters of AI integration, it is essential to persistently question, regulate and learn. Each step we take towards embracing AI should be accompanied by one deep pondering its implications for the legal, ethical, economic, and social fabric of our existence.

Chapter 10. Societal Shifts: Changing Cultures and Communities

In the thrilling narrative of technology and humanity's evolution, one of the most valuable pieces to consider involves profound societal shifts occurring due to the advancements made in both hardware and software facets of our perceived reality. These changes, as subtle as they might be today, bear the potential to reshape cultures, communities, and the very fabric that binds our society.

10.1. The Confluence of Technology and Culture

Traditions, shared values, and cultural practices have long been instrumental in shaping societies. However, the adoption of technology, specifically those powered by artificial intelligence (AI), make an impact of such magnitude, altering cultural developments and societal norms. From shaping our interaction with the world to transforming our perceptions and expectations, technology's influence is pervasive.

Social media platforms have been one of the most visible reflections of these changes. It has not only transformed communication norms but has inadvertently created a new, global culture where sharing, liking, following, and commenting are universally understood actions. Powered by AI and big data, social media not only offers an accessible and engaging platform for expression but also subtly shapes users' behavior, their ideas about privacy, and even their mental health.

Artificial Intelligence (AI) has also begun to redefine art and creativity. AI programs compose music, design artworks, and even write poetry, challenging humans' monopoly on creativity. But beyond mere competition, the interaction of AI and art is sparking a cultural conversation around the definition of creativity, originality, and the very essence of art.

10.2. Technology-driven Shift in Communities

As technology stretches its tendrils into our day-to-day lives, communities too evolve and adapt to cater to this seismic shift. Online communities, circumventing geographical borders, have fostered a sense of shared values and interests, effectively piercing the confines of traditional community lines.

Augmented Reality (AR) and Virtual Reality (VR) are two emerging technological fields with unparalleled potential to remodel community interaction. They blur the line between digital and physical space, redefining concepts like proximity and location, paving the way for even more vibrant, versatile virtual communities. These virtual communities, reinforced by reciprocal action and common objectives, could potentially harbor strong emotional ties and community sentiments parallel to physical communities.

Technology has also drastically shaped the dynamics of the workforce community. The rise of remote work and digital nomadism activities, facilitated by technological tools, has reimagined workplace culture, powered by digital transformation. Veritably, the future of work could easily be community-oriented, empowered by collaborative tools and platforms, transcending physical boundaries, and united by their shared professional interests.

10.3. The Ethical Questions and Societal Challenges

In this rapid stride towards technological singularity, ethics and societal challenges should be center stage. From privacy concerns magnified by AI and Big Data to the digital divide segregating the technologically proficient from the rest, the road to Technological Singularity is not without its thorns.

Emerging technologies such as AI and automation pose significant challenges to labor markets, with the potential to lead to job displacement and increased inequality. Nations need to address such disparities and ensure no one is left behind in this technological leap. It implies reforming education systems to arm future generations with the skills needed in a rapidly changing job market.

Additionally, the merging of the digital and physical worlds raises questions of cybersecurity, privacy, and identity. With personal data becoming a new currency, societies need to balance the convenience of technology with the protection of individual privacy. The rise of deepfakes, AI-generated synthetic media representing real individuals, calls for innovative solutions to maintain the sanctity of truth in the digital era.

10.4. Towards a Shared Future

Undeniably, the integration of AI into societal structures will profoundly impact cultures and communities, for better or worse. However, one dominant thread weaves this complex tapestry: that technology is a tool. It's a means to an end, combining the far-stretching potential of AI with the richness of human thought, creativity, and understanding.

A successful societal shift does not end with the widespread adoption of AI. Success lies in synchronizing this adoption with a deep understanding of culturally sensitive AI, maintaining inclusivity, protecting privacy, and fostering shared values. The future we imagine, with humans and machines coexisting in harmony, necessitates more than just technological advancement—it requires a shared vision, a collective leap towards a converging horizon in the realm of singularity.

At the crossroads of human evolution and technological advancement, we stand, ready to create, ready to adapt, and ready to leap towards this new era. An era where cultures morph, communities evolve, societies transform, and what it means to be human could be beautifully redefined.

In the grand narrative of the Singularity, it's not the end that matters—it's the journey, the understanding, and the collective decision to shape a future that benefits humanity as a whole. The Singularity, intriguing as it may be, is the next chapter of man's evolution—a testament to our intelligence, adaptability, and shared will to overturn long-standing paradigms.

Chapter 11. Predicted Trajectories: Mapping the Onset of The Singularity

It is crucial first to establish a solid understanding of the concept of singularity. Coined in 1958 by mathematician John von Neumann, 'Singularity' in the context of futurism refers to a point in time where technological growth becomes uncontrollable and irreversible, thereby causing unimaginable changes to human civilization. This phenomenological crossroads has been the topic of extensive deliberations by researchers, scientists, futurists, and philosophers alike.

11.1. The Quantum Leap in Technology

Let's begin with the exponential progression of technology. Moore's law predicts that the number of transistors on integrated circuits doubles approximately every two years. While Moore's law predominantly focuses on hardware, similar trends are visible within the realms of software and algorithms. This not only implies rapid technological advancement but suggests that within several decades, we could witness a meshing of human consciousness and machine intelligence, leading to the singularity.

A glimpse of this future is already evident in brain-computer interfaces (BCI), nanotechnology, and quantum computing. We're gradually moving past the age of digital computing into the dawn of quantum computation which promises to speed up computation immeasurably. Innovative efforts in creating quantum computer architectures and quantum algorithm design can lead us to this future faster than ever expected.

11.2. Artificial Superintelligence: A Major Catalyst

Artificial Superintelligence (ASI) is the magnifying glass that could catalyze singularity. ASI, an intellect that is much smarter than the best human brains in practically every field, including scientific creativity, general wisdom, and social skills, is currently the focal point of intense research and development.

Ray Kurzweil, a prominent futurist, predicted that an AI will pass the Turing test by 2029, showcasing a machine's ability to exhibit intelligent behavior equivalent to, or indistinguishable from, human behavior. The inception of an ASI era will fundamentally reshape our world, where machines continually improve themselves, leading to an 'intelligence explosion', and the unstoppable advent of singularity.

11.3. The Aging Paradox & Transhumanism

Simultaneously, biotechnology advances have led to increased average life spans, bringing us to an aging paradox where our ability to extend life meets our inability to substantially improve the quality of life for the aged. However, transhumanism proposes drastic possibilities, such as uploading human consciousness into a digital platform, to navigate this challenge.

Transhumanists imagine a future where human existence is no longer confined within biological boundaries. So, what happens when these artificial entities outlive their creators? Predicting the outset of singularity thus involves understanding these emerging trends in biotechnology, longevity studies, and their intersection with AI.

11.4. Roadmap to Singularity: Timeframes and Predictions

Estimating the exact timeline for the onset of the singularity remains challenging. However, researchers like Ray Kurzweil predict the singularity to occur around 2045, while others propose a timeline that extends well into the latter part of the century.

In a survey by AI experts, the median year predicted for "high-level machine intelligence" to perform most economically relevant intellectual tasks as humans do was 2040-2050. However, given the high-risk nature of these predictions, many experts urge proactive anticipatory strategies to prepare for the immense future uncertainties.

11.5. Debates and Divergence: The Obstacles Ahead

While some hail the singularity as our destiny, others debate its timing or challenge its inevitability altogether. Technological progress can be stalled by socio-political barriers, financial constraints, or the creation of ASI might be far more complex than we currently understand. In confronting singularity, we can't afford to ignore the ethical and societal implications, which will be as influential as the technological determinants.

11.6. Towards a Singularity: Paradigm Shift

As our civilization teeters on the edge of this technological revolution, the trajectory towards the singularity points towards a fundamental shift in our existence, an alteration in the human experience as we know it. The onset of singularity, when it occurs, will reconfigure our perspectives on humanity, ethics, governance, personal identity, and consciousness.

In conclusion, predicting the trajectory and onset of the singularity involves an integral study of the present and careful extrapolation of future trends. At the intersection of technology and philosophy, the journey towards singularity is paved with fascinating possibilities and enticing opportunities. Our future is at stake, and the singularity could be the most significant turn in human evolution since the dawn of consciousness itself.

Chapter 12. Beyond the Singularity: Exploring Post-Human Futures

The concept of the singularity, the moment when technological advancement outpaces human comprehension or control, raises fundamental questions about the trajectory of human evolution and our role in shaping the future. What will the post-human world look like and how will we navigate its unfamiliar territory? Let's begin our exploration.

12.1. Life After the Singularity: A Speculative Vision

Technological Singularitarianists, such as Ray Kurzweil, propose that post-Singularity AI will far surpass our current understanding, turning into a sort of technologically advanced "gods" or superintelligences. These entities can resemble humans in form and function or can exist as something entirely new and incomprehensible to human minds.

Robotic bodies may become the norm, no longer restricted by biological limitations. Death, as we understand it, could become obsolete as minds are uploaded into resilient technological substrates. We may see societies where flesh and blood humans coexist with cybernetic organisms, and synthetic consciousness exists in the cloud.

12.2. Ethical Considerations and Post-Human Rights

In a post-Singularity world, issues of ethics and rights could stretch our philosophical frameworks to their limits. As AI develops awareness and consciousness, should they be granted rights? Will conventional definitions of identity, sentient being, and life hold ground?

Comparative forays into animal rights and legal rights of natural resources can provide some groundwork. Yet, such analogies fall short in addressing the profound shift in understanding life and personhood that the singularity can bring about.

12.3. Re-defining Reality in the Post-Singularity World

Are humans prepared to redefine their reality? AI-driven virtual and augmented reality technologies could blur the lines between the real and the digital so finely that distinguishing between the two becomes challenging. Immersive virtual worlds could bring their custom laws of physics, allowing individuals to experience realities beyond human comprehension or replication, offering a canvas for living the lives we dreamt of, free from physical constraints.

12.4. The Economy of a Post-Human Future

What happens to the economy when we cross the Singularity? In an era where machines are more innovative, skilled, and productive than humans, traditional economic concepts such as labor, capital, and markets may be obsolete.

One possible outcome is a radical shift from capitalism to an economy based on abundance, where growth is no longer driven by human labor and natural resources. Instead, digital services and AI-generated goods become the primary commodities, with distribution and access posing new challenges and generating conflict.

12.5. Human Evolution: Genetically Modified Humans

Genetic engineering, driven by advancements in AI, can lead to a new generation of humans more adept to survive in a technological society while influencing the course of biological evolution. There may come a time when natural selection gives way to artificial variation and selection, leading to an entirely new spectrum of human-constructed species, potentially alongside those resulting from AI itself.

In this narrative, the relevance of Darwinian evolution comes under question, and a new evolutionary framework based on information and artificial creation could be the norm.

12.6. Concluding Thoughts on the Post-Singularity Landscape

Mapping out different possibilities about the post-Singularity world is not an attempt to predict the future in absolute terms; it is, instead, an exercise in facilitating our readiness for a world we can scarcely imagine post the Singularity. The future will likely surprise us, irrespective of how accurately we anticipate it. However, such speculation is beneficial in equipping us with the mental flexibility needed to navigate the immense changes that the Singularity, if it transpires as forecasted, would bring.

In so doing, we shape our minds to be at ease with continual radical change - a requisite skill in a post-Singularity era. What is most crucial is not the precise details of the emerging landscape but the mental adaptability to confront, comprehend, and guide it. For humanity to traverse the singularity with grace and wisdom, we must ensure that our hearts and minds move in harmony with the pace of technological advancement.

While the singularity might represent the limits of our current understanding, it does not symbolize an end in itself. Rather, it is a passage from which a post-human existence unfolds—an existence marked not by human-centric paradigms, but by a universe made diverse and richer through our scientific and technological breakthroughs.